# A Yellow Spoon

Hannie Schaft

BookLeaf
Publishing

India | USA | UK

Presentation by *BookLeaf Publishing*

Web: www.bookleafpub.com

E-mail: info@bookleafpub.com

ISBN: 9789360943813

First edition 2024

# DEDICATION

*To my favorite kids.*

*We are indomitable.*

# ACKNOWLEDGEMENT

With admiration for Jamie, who saw them first.
With love for Sara, who always saw the best.
With great admiration for Mary Oliver, who showed me the music of words.

# PREFACE

Hannie **Schaft** was the infamous Dutch resistance fighter known as "the girl with the red hair" during WWII. For her work in the resistance, Schaft was executed by Dutch Nazi officials on April 17, 1945. She was shot in the head, but the bullet only grazed Schaft. She allegedly told her executioners: *Ik schiet beter* "I shoot better!" A final shot to her head ended her life, but not her incredible legacy.[5][8]

# I Can't Write Poetry

"What if," he said,
"Every poet thought:
"I can't write poetry, it won't sell!"

I wondered
if Emily ever doubted, or if she Knew;
Byron, I'm sure, would never be
so gauche as to think of money
Lord Tennyson never worried about rent

I am sure Mary Oliver had moments
at the shore
or in a meadow
and I wish I could sit
beneath the spreading trees
and ask her where she put
the imposter qualms.

# DELETE

There must have been moments
when Browning
tore everything asunder;
threw it onto a glowing grate
and watched the ink run,
the letters curl and burn.
It must have been so much more satisfying than
"DELETE".

# Chronic

"OH!"
He blushed. "Sorry, that was unprofessional."
The nurse stared at my chart again.
"I was just… shocked. You're so young!"

"Yeah,"
I plastered my best smile,
"I am attempting to collect
every diagnosis."
We laughed.

I didn't say,
"I can't remember anymore
when I wasn't
in pain."

# Snow White

Tall, glass ceilings only exist
for the girls who dare to look up.

Some of us pose in glass displays
worshipped, untouched, coated in dust.

Glass ceilings; the greenhouse effect
beckons us to rise with courage -

But how will we bathe in sunlight
when our eyes are closed?
I wonder

Some of us lie in glass coffins
waiting for permission to wake.

# You are Not Drowning

You are not drowning
in the pounding heart
   of the wave

You lie in wait
Pummeled by the riptide,
   limp against the current

But this wave will soon be spent
See? Its deep power fades
   the crushing pressure relents

Then
Then, you swim
Fight for the surface
Kick and claw, but wait
   for now

You must not fight the wave
Let it have its way, for a time
It is only a wave
You have ridden a thousand before
There are a thousand more
It is only a wave
   and it must pass

You endure;
In the vast ocean
    this is only a wave


                Wait

# Misanthropy

We stood in your ranks,
bound by chromosomes.
You betrayed us in the heat of battle;
your war crimes sullied our ideals.

Narcissus looks away
for You are more cruel than Fates.

We, who have suffered,
we rallied for Truth,
and raised bloodied faces to
defend your craven campaign.

We seethe.

Now,
we see you,
we declare that you are no Woman.
You cry for sympathy
from the very ones you shame -
how dare you lie about the violence
We survived
as if it were your own.

You eat your sons, as the Titan,
Chronos, and

sacrifice your daughters to Furies.
You are no Amazon;
you are the Abomination.
you betrayed the wounded, you are Kakia.[1]

In Greek mythology, Kakia (Cacia in Latin) was the
goddess of vice and moral decay.

----

[1]

# Memorial

You don't need to remember
Every struggle, every hurt
Or how you survived

Hoarding memories to prove it happened
Lying awake to count each loss.

You can lay them down
And walk away, into the new
Your sorrows will not be lost

I'll remember for you
I'll carve the victories in stone
The Homer to your Odyssey

Sail toward that horizon
And never fear
Being forgotten
The sirens will forever sing of you.

# Archy & Mehitabel

I heard a story - I was young -
an epistolary tale between
a cat and a roach:

The roach told of a moth's demise
it fought to reach its great love, a candle,
and perished; I cried.

The roach wrote that the moth was a fool
and yet, wished he might desire
anything
enough to be burned

I always wondered, what a cat would respond.

Indifference is safe, but even a cockroach

envies passion.

# It's Time to Leave the Woods

I.
I flew over brick walks,
the moment I realized
I wanted you.
after three years of pursuit
I was the one running
(which seems only fair)
and I ran to find you
in that dusty library, lost in a book.
We went to the quiet concert hall,
and I tried to explain -
over my thundering heart -
your nose did that bewildered wrinkle
and my courage failed me
"Nevermind! A joke!" -
but you took my hand and told me to shut up
and smiled at me.
We sat on the stage and swung our legs
blushed, giddy,
while the Steinways eavesdropped.

II.
Blonde, spiky head peered around the door,
you watched me wrestle with Brahms.
You splayed gangly legs over
the ancient chair and listened.

I missed the leap, F# to A, again and again.
"Why jump?" you asked.
"My hand is too small," I confessed.
You stood, "Try like this",
dropped your wide hand over mine;
long, elegant fingers
played both notes with ease.

I remember the fury;
I told you:
"Get out".

And that was how we met.

III.


Sondheim understood:
"I never thought I could be so happy".
We danced in the finale;
my Baker's Wife skirt tangled in
the cape of your Mysterious Man.

I resented the lyrics, then;
too saccharine for my twenty-one years.
I didn't understand how the Woods
could change a tale;
after the tasks and witch and cow,
I believed we had earned
happily ever after.

But Stephen knew: "Sometimes, people leave
you, halfway through the wood".

# Cockroach

There - wriggling on her back - six legs
Seek purchase in the cold, dry air.
I pause beside her. Empathy
Is heavier than I can bear.

She flails, supine, on carpet worn
a martyr in this hallowed hall.
I am upended, just like her;
I panic, maddened by the fall.

We break for freedom! In my hands,
escape into the glaring sun.
Her feet find earth, my knees find grass,
I see I'm not the only one.

# Ukelele

He had your nose before he was born;

Soon, he toddled to the shelf to
peruse Chopin;
chubby fingers mashed the keys
when you played Scriabin.
"This is Jeopardy!" he crowed and clapped.

But then, you disappeared;
he worried about rent, compound interest,-
he slept on the cot
so his sister wouldn't be afraid.

I watch him open jars for her,
make puns, play the piano
with your long fingers.

I thought I knew you,
but the betrayal of our vows
is as nothing to this -
you missed the day our son learned
his sister's favorite song
and played his ukelele
so she could sing.

# Shrapnel

Festering splinters that break tender skin
Red, swollen shards I feel rising within
Once, it was merely a scent in a park
Memories crowded, both lovely and dark.
Then, you were met as a ghost in my room;
Crying for futures your absence consumed.
Weeping each autumn, I pick at my scars
Dreading, yet craving, those lifetimes of ours
Lived in a love that fades more every year.
Can it be shrapnel is mutual, my dear?

Time paints betrayal in soft hues of gray,
But when I dislodge detritus each day,
The colors are vivid, and I, at your feet
Bleed with desire, for promises sweet.

Sometimes, I breathe and forget what you said,
I don't lie awake with your voice in my head…
Then, in my new joy, I feel the sharp bite -
Of longings I thought were all put to flight.
How long - do you know? - until I am free?
For long, dead love itches -

or is it just me?

# The Long War

Christmases gone haunt our stockings each year,
those holidays past you have missed,
Squeals of our children, their laughter and tears,
your cruelties are such a long list.

I lost more than family, lost dearer friends,
I hung all the lights on my own.
You missed the growth spurts to chase your own
ends,
and six awful years have now flown.

Sometimes, I miss you, resent you, or weep,
I ponder on what might have been -
Our kids come to me with joys and grief deep,
I'm glad I kept my vows to them.

For your sake, I hope the loss was worthwhile -
Because when it's all said and done,
I got the tears and the everyday smiles,
You lose - the long war has been won.

# Free Range

I envy the other chattel
for beasts may gaze upon nature
and wonder
but I must measure every thought against
the Rod.


I would crawl on all fours
if I might be free to
choose my own grass.

# Shattered

I broke a crystal vase;
Shards too small to heal
Powdered bits of shining,
bleeding,　　　cutting
edges


I cannot ever find them all.

And this is how you left me.

# Insatiable

In the night, I wake hungry
and I crave your voice
I wander to the kitchen, hunting
but a banana, at 3am,
isn't your embrace
and I am starving
for your hands on my hips
your lips on my neck
I lie in the dark

Insatiable

# Bird

There is this f-cking bird
It's right outside my window
He sings of spring and joy
while I lie in the dark, and -

Beneath the weight I can't quite catch my breath
for fear that Reality will find us,
me and Grief, and smother -

This fucking bird goes on
He chirps and soars while I clutch at blankets
wondering if painting all the things yellow
will ease the cold screws twisting in my chest

But I can't paint or eat
unless I leave my nest of Pillows and Darkness
and I can't bear to leave or be left anymore

even by the fucking bird.

# I Sail

You breathe, and I, small bark,
Am drawn into the lee of wind
Your arms

I rise and fall; a ship
Upon the sea of your
Embrace

Your supple skin frames all
The world I crave to drown
Within

And so, I stretch my hand
My fingers ache for you
Entwine

Frail bodies keep our shores
Apart; yet longing, I
Sail on

Forever seeking where
Our waters may collide
Engulf

# Princess

I still tell stories of you and of me -
Twenty-four years' worth of tales
Legends we authored and myths of the sea
Spun while we wandered old trails.

Comrades, shared secrets and fears late at night,
We were more sisters than friends.
Shared every triumph and fall as we grew,
Huddled with weathered bookends.

Characters drawn and the plots oft revised,
Life and our fictions were blurred.
I grew, faced trials, found courage, devised -
Clean fairy tales you preferred.

I miss the fantasies, perfect and bright
My world has Real bills to pay,
I'm glad your castle and bubble are tight
You cannot see me this way

I know I'm not special, you've cut scenes before,
Edits are part of the charm.
Subplots that don't fit lie cut on the floor,
Can't bring your paradise harm.

# Symphony No. 4

We walked in the thunder and rain
after Brahms,
symphony echoes alive in the park.
You were too stubborn to share an umbrella,
so, splashing in puddles, I ruined my yellow
shoes.

The symphony in E minor still takes me back
to the petrichor of that tropical storm;
the rain on your glasses, and
the goosebumps on my arm.

I was pulled into your orbit that night,
and danced in the eye

but the cruelest weather was
after the hurricane;
I watched the currents pull you away.

I lie on my side with splintered ribs,
my tattered hull choked in sand,
a derelict ship
forgotten by your sea.

# Fibonacci

25

Craft
in
every
spiral conch
Golden ratio,
etched in art, music, and pinecones,
By what power were you cast to every stage on
Earth?

# Remnants



I wanted to be enough,
but I bruise too easily.
I wanted to be brave,
but I jolt awake, cold with sweat,
afraid of you.
I'm sorry that we met
and, bloodied with pain,
tried to bind our wounds
with the tattered remnants
of each other.

# Valentine

These tears are for the red card you gave me
today,
for the valentines I want to forget.
these burning, bewildered tears are for forehead
kisses and winter afternoon naps and promises
unkept,
gifts from every Love that broke me in a new
way.
This is the first, long love letter you've
composed for me - and silly me -
I cry, wondering if
someday, I'll hide this beautiful, tender missive
in the back of a drawer,
in the quiet grave with the others,
to be exhumed every year
for a fresh autopsy
and wept over again.

# Cassandra

I know that I'm an asshole, friend -
But when have I been wrong?
An oracle of mundane dross,
Composing plangent song
I take no joy in being right.
I wish that tales were true.
If I could blind myself to Truth,
I'd build a myth for you.

# David

He was my king.
I bathed within his gaze,
Drew breath from every word,
And in his arms

I was a queen.
His passion broke my deep resolve,
And lost in his embrace I found
The puzzle piece

That fit, just right.
And finally, I slept in peace, and woke
to find his arms replaced with shackles,
An iron grip.

He did not need
To clutch and grasp and claw.
I would have rested gently
On his shoulder.

# Rite of Spring

A Monday, once, was blue,
blustery with frost,
Anticipating blossoms.

Sparrows in the naked maple
Dart and dance;
Their sacred rite invites the sun.
Finches sing incantations to
Dormant azaleas

A robin on the blue gray roof
Calls to the oak,
Encouraging crimson buds to
"Grow! Grow!... grow!...."

Come, summer, come!
We wait, breathless with hope, the
Weary birds and I.

# Kintsugi

Everyone is out
looking for themselves,
with trowels and flashlights
maps drawn by therapists,
as if the perfect self
is waiting to be found -
like a lost earring.
I am certain that my search will be
an ancient, interminable
archeological dig, requiring
years of work and special tools
to brush and measure,
gently excavate,
inch by inch.
Beneath the dirt and legends and curses
and the refuse of modernity,
loving hands will lift a fragment
and we will celebrate with joy;
each new piece laid,
with painstaking care,
among the broken bits
until they can be repaired
with gold.

# RAZOR

I offer my memories on a cold, porcelain altar.
We sit on the lip of the tub,
with painted toes in warm water,
while I show her how to shave
gently, around the ankle
carefully, over the knee
my baby, wearing a young woman's face,
peppers me with curiosity,
little knowing that she breaks
a family curse with every giggle.

When I was fifteen, I begged for a razor.
I was the only girl I knew
who hid hairy legs by sitting on my knees
my mother cried and said
that shaved legs invited pedophiles.
I hid in the bathroom,
ashamed my growing made her cry.
No one saw me bleed
from the hundred tiny cuts.

We sit on the altar and
my girl laughs at the awkward ritual.
She says, "Eh, it's only a little blood. I'll be
fine."

# Estranged

*with Sara*

Love, don't cry -
The cruel patterns they wove
Won't hold.
Truth
Leaks through the slats;
All those iron lies
Rust beneath the drip of reality's grief.
Moths nibble edges of
Mouldering misunderstandings
Curious fingers work at the holes
Unknot the bitter tangles
Until
One gentle pull
On a single thread
Unravels the whole and
Reveals the gold of your
Love.

# Iambs

I wish that I could write the way
The famous poets do;
Without a meter, rhyme, or plan,
And to my madness give no clue,


But when I read the paeons old,
Their lilts and cadence, rhythms call;
I am seduced by sonnets bold,
I long for words to rise and fall.


The more fool, I, for now I dance
Attendance on a stoic god;
My feeble words, beneath Their glance,
Are measured by syllabic rods.


I ache for freedom, envious
Of laureates who write so free;
But in my soul, all verse is song,
I can't deny the melody.

# NAIVE

I thought that evidence would win,
I thought, with truth in hand;
But I, the woman, steeped in "sin",
Bewildered, could not understand -


That right or wrong was not the key.
The Church would not abide,
A cry for mercy, not from me,
When once I stepped outside.


I faced the wilderness with tears,
I hoped for justice swift,
I learned to live with my worst fears,
the wrong side of the rift.


But joy comes in the morning, see,
You must not fear the night
The truth will set your spirit free
When you trade lies for light.

# HEART

Love is not
A lightning strike;
The One never existed and never will
Because Love is everywhere.
It grows in cracked sidewalks
Like weeds that flower,
It builds webs in the corners of soft places
And sparkles with dew at dawn.


Love blooms in the detritus of expectations
And its tendrils caress the ambivalent.


The fairy tale isn't over;
Happily is found in ever after,
Every day,
Wherever dappled shadows seduce
And a single glance frees the heart
To hope.

# FLOWERS

I lay shriveled, pink carnations
on the grave of the woman
I used to be
She cut coupons and prayed
and sewed kids' clothes and volunteered
and tried so hard.
I refresh the peonies
by the urn of the woman
I thought I'd be
She would have been the very best church wife
her husband would have prized her above rubies
her children were meant to be numerous.
Now, I water dandelion and chrysanthemum
I tame the hellebore
and I cherish the woman
who made it this far;
the cherry tree that I planted
blooms larger
every year

# BREATHE

"I'm scared," I said.

"I'm scared, too," he said.

"I grew up with Anger," I said. "It's not good for our kids. But, we can fix this. You need help. And I promise, I'll go with you."

Sigh. "I don't want people to think I'm an abusive person," he said.

I paused. Then I tried:

"I went to therapy for years because you said I was broken.

I gave up our church when you said you wanted out.

I gave up jobs, because I would do anything to make this work.

It never occurred to me to worry what other people might think

- because I loved you.

I was terrified of losing Us."

"Oh," he said. "That, too. I mean, I worry about that, too."

"I have to go." I couldn't speak after I hung up. She came in and saw my face. I cannot forget hers.

"Oh, honey," she whispered, "How could he Not love you??"

I don't remember much.

Her arms were around me and she said,
"Breathe, breathe! You must breathe."
And I tried, between the sobs.
I tried to breathe
But there wasn't any air left.

# COMPOST

They say that eggshells
are excellent fertilizers.
so, I took our detritus,
left over from a decade of tiptoeing
and crushed them
in the same, strong fingers
that planted fresh herbs
I scattered the shells
at the roots of my garden
and watched the new sprouts
thrive.

# BETTER

41

You placed your hands on my hips.
"Hold on to my neck," you whispered.
And gently, slowly, you lowered me to the
mountain of couch cushions.
"Can't she sit down on her own?" a kid
demanded.
You chuckled. "She can," you said, "But her
back hurts. I know how that feels. I want to
help."
You put pillows under my knees.
"Better?"
And it was.

# Divinity

If there is a God,
they live within the
happy, thumping tail
of a deaf dog,
in the silence between the second
and third movements,
in the slack jaws of sleeping children
who grip my neck to be carried inside
and never miss a wink

in the wet dirt
with tiny herbs
on the cusp of overthrowing the garden,
in the last moments
with silky, frail hands clasping mine

in the way a sullen teenager
can fire barbs at random,
carry a thundercloud throughout the house,
and yet,
without warning
pierce you with a stare to say,
"You know you're amazing, right?"

# Indelible

They are scratched on the walls
in the darkest shadows of my mind,
Words, spoken to me, that time cannot erase:

"You're a monster."
"Why are you so weird?"
"If you were a boy, your grandfather would have
loved you."
"You are Indomitable."

"Frankly, your story is hard to believe."
"God is punishing you."

"Mom, will you tuck me in?"
"You're the best teacher!"
"Are we poor now?"
"You're my hero."
"Your enthusiasm intimidates some people."
"You're hired!"
"We're letting you go."

"I'll always be here for you."
"I have to move away."

"It's a brain tumor."

"Let the men talk to the men. We know your skills."
"I'm sorry I frightened you."
"Why would I want you after that?"

"Are you overreacting because your parents beat you?"
"Are you crying because he cheated on you?"

"I'm sorry. You tried to tell us,
and we didn't believe you."
"Take some time and get over it."
"You were right."
"I hate when you are right."

"I love you."

"Bitch."

# Forty

Here is a list of all the things I have
Tattooed on my soul
After forty years:

The smile on my best friend's face,
When I woke up from surgery.
The expression on my dog's face,
when he knew I was his home.

The sound of the Steinway
When my first love played Chopin;
The tone of his voice a decade later:
"You'd be fine if I left you."

The taste of the quiche I destroyed
With graham cracker crust,
The flavor of a sake bomb,
To drown the grief of divorce.

The scent of my grandmother,
Lavender hugs and the coal stove,
The smell of my girlie's hair
When we read books before bed.

The butterfly flutters of a baby in my stomach,
The cold sweat of waking alone,
The sharp edges of the ring I gave back.

The voices of my chorus students,
The laughter of my giddy kids,
The soft gloaming in my garden
And the meteor shower in a cold, black night -

"Somewhere Over the Rainbow"
On the ukelele.
A wet road trip to Maine;
A cold key, to my own house,
In my own hand.

Barefoot in the grass,
soaking up green mountains,
While she runs in happy circles,
Shouting, "This is the
Most perfect day!"

www.ingramcontent.com/pod-product-compliance
Lightning Source LLC
LaVergne TN
LVHW041237200726
843507LV00013B/2722